Startup Symphony

Making the Most of Your Early Years

Abhay Raj Solanki

Founder & CEO, Suman Publications

Suman Publications Private Limited

B017, Sigma III, Greater Noida

Uttar Pradesh – 201310, INDIA

www.sumanpublications.com

Published by Suman Publications

ISBN: 978-81-973674-1-0

Cover Design by Shruti Gontla

Inside book formatting and typesetting by Suman Publications

Printed at Repro India Limited, Mumbai

First Edition Published in 2025

INTRODUCTION

Tuning Your Startup Symphony

The Entrepreneurial Spark

Every great symphony begins with a single note, and every successful startup begins with a single spark. For many young entrepreneurs, that spark is a problem they can't stop thinking about, an idea they believe can change the world, or a deep desire to create something meaningful.

This book is your guide to harnessing that spark and turning it into a harmonious symphony—a thriving startup that not only survives the challenges of the early years but also flourishes into a lasting legacy.

Why Startups Are Like Symphonies

A startup, much like a symphony, requires harmony among its many components. The visionary entrepreneur plays the role of the conductor, bringing together diverse elements: the team, the product, the market, and the strategy. Each part must work together seamlessly to create a masterpiece.

However, as in any symphony, there will be moments of discord. Instruments might go out of tune, or the tempo might falter. Your ability to navigate these challenges will determine whether your startup can rise to its full potential. This book is designed to help you find your rhythm, overcome setbacks, and create a startup that resonates with success.

What This Book Will Teach You

In the chapters ahead, you'll learn how to:

- Build a strong foundation for your startup.
- Navigate the challenges of early-stage entrepreneurship.
- Grow and scale your business while staying true to your vision.
- Cultivate resilience and adapt to an ever-changing business landscape.

Whether you're at the idea stage or already running a fledgling startup, this book will provide the insights and tools you need to make the most of your early years.

Acknowledgment

This book is the culmination of countless interactions, invaluable lessons, and the unyielding support of a vibrant entrepreneurial ecosystem. Writing *Startup Symphony* has been a journey of reflection, growth, and collaboration, and I am deeply grateful to everyone who has played a part in shaping it.

To the many entrepreneurs, mentors, and visionaries I've had the privilege to meet, thank you for sharing your stories, struggles, and successes. Your experiences have added richness and depth to this narrative.

To my family and friends, your unwavering belief in me has been my greatest source of strength. Your encouragement and love have fueled my passion and perseverance.

Finally, to the readers of this book, thank you for embarking on this journey with me. May *Startup Symphony* inspire you to compose your unique entrepreneurial masterpiece.

With gratitude,
Abhay Raj Solanki

About the Author

Abhay Raj Solanki is the visionary Founder & CEO of Suman Publications, one of India's fastest-growing publishing houses. A passionate advocate for entrepreneurship and creativity, he has collaborated with over 500 budding authors, helping them bring their ideas to life.

With years of experience navigating the complexities of startup culture, Abhay Raj has dedicated his career to empowering entrepreneurs to turn their ideas into thriving businesses. His unique perspective blends practical strategies with an empathetic understanding of the challenges entrepreneurs face.

Through *Startup Symphony*, Abhay Raj shares not just a roadmap for business success but also a celebration of resilience, vision, and the entrepreneurial spirit.

Reader's Note

Dear Reader,

Welcome to *Startup Symphony*. Whether you're an aspiring entrepreneur, a founder navigating the early stages of your business, or a seasoned innovator seeking fresh insights, this book is crafted with you in mind.

Entrepreneurship is a journey, and like a symphony, it's a blend of harmony, creativity, and precision. Each chapter is designed to guide you through the key movements of building and scaling a successful startup, offering practical strategies, inspiring stories, and actionable exercises.

This book is not meant to be read in a single sitting. Treat it as a companion for your entrepreneurial journey. Feel free to explore chapters based on where you currently stand—whether it's finding your startup's rhythm, assembling a dream team, or overcoming discord and setbacks.

At the end of each chapter, you'll find reflection questions and exercises to help you internalize the lessons and apply them to your unique situation. Take your time with these—they're designed to turn insights into action.

As you embark on this adventure, remember that every entrepreneur faces challenges, moments of self-doubt, and unexpected twists. But these are also opportunities for growth and innovation. My hope is that *Startup Symphony* not only equips you with tools for success but also inspires you to embrace the journey with passion and resilience.

Here's to orchestrating your masterpiece. Let the symphony begin!

Index

1

The Startup Mindset

Every journey begins with the right mindset. Successful entrepreneurs share a set of traits that enable them to overcome challenges, embrace innovation, and stay committed to their goals.

The Traits of Successful Entrepreneurs

1. **Visionary Thinking:** The ability to see the big picture and anticipate trends. For instance, consider how Elon Musk envisioned electric vehicles becoming mainstream long before the world was ready for Tesla.

2. **Resilience:** A willingness to keep going despite setbacks. J.K. Rowling faced rejection from 12 publishers before *Harry Potter* became a global phenomenon. [illegible] to thrive unde

3. **Adaptability:** Being open to change and ready to pivot when necessary. Netflix started as a DVD rental company and transformed into a global streaming giant when they saw the market shifting.

4. **Curiosity:** A constant desire to learn and grow. Successful entrepreneurs never stop asking questions and seeking new knowledge, much like Steve Jobs, who continuously innovated at Apple.

5. **Optimism:** Believing in the possibility of success even in the face of doubt. Optimism is contagious and can inspire teams to persevere even during tough times.

How to Cultivate the Startup Mindset

Developing these traits is a continuous process. Start by setting clear goals and visualizing your success. Surround yourself with positive influences, seek out mentors, and embrace failure as a learning opportunity.

Building the right mindset also involves developing emotional intelligence. This includes being self-aware, managing your emotions, and understanding the perspectives of others. For example, Sara Blakely, the founder of Spanx, often credits her emotional resilience and ability to empathize with her customers for her success.

Personal Story: Embracing Failure as a Stepping Stone

When I first started my entrepreneurial journey, I faced self-doubt. My first venture, a small tech services company, struggled to find clients. I remember spending countless nights rethinking my approach. One day, a mentor told me, “Failures are just steps on the staircase to success.” That advice pushed me to pivot and focus on smaller, manageable goals. Within a year, we landed our first big client. That lesson—resilience and adaptability—became the cornerstone of my entrepreneurial mindset.

A Deep Dive: The Power of Optimism

Optimism isn’t just about a positive attitude; it’s about expecting the best outcomes while preparing for the worst. Research shows that optimistic leaders are more likely to inspire confidence in their teams. A study by Harvard Business Review found that teams led by optimistic leaders reported 31% higher productivity.

Imagine a startup team working on a revolutionary app for mental health. They face multiple technical glitches and regulatory hurdles. Their leader, however, keeps reiterating the impact this app could have on millions of users. This optimism fuels the team's efforts, keeping morale high and inspiring innovative solutions.

Practical Exercises to Build a Startup Mindset

1. **Vision Board:** Create a visual representation of your goals. Include images, quotes, and milestones you want to achieve.
2. **Resilience Training:** Write down three recent challenges and list how you overcame or learned from them. Reflect on what strategies worked and how you can apply them in the future.
3. **Daily Curiosity Practice:** Set aside 15 minutes each day to learn something new about your industry or a related field.

Case Study: Turning Setbacks into Comebacks

Consider the story of Slack, the popular communication platform. Before becoming a billion-dollar company, the founders created a gaming platform that failed miserably. Instead of giving up, they repurposed the internal communication tool they had built for their team, which became Slack. Their ability to adapt and maintain a growth mindset transformed failure into an opportunity.

Reflection Questions

- What is your vision for your startup, and how can you break it into smaller, actionable goals?
- How do you respond to setbacks? What steps can you take to build resilience?
- Who inspires you as an entrepreneur, and what traits do they embody that you can emulate?

Expanding Emotional Intelligence for Leadership

Emotional intelligence is a cornerstone of effective leadership. Entrepreneurs often juggle multiple roles, requiring them to manage not only their emotions but also the dynamics within their team.

The Five Pillars of Emotional Intelligence:

1. **Self-Awareness:** Understanding your emotions and how they impact your decisions.
2. **Self-Regulation:** Managing emotions constructively.
3. **Motivation:** Staying driven by internal rewards rather than external pressures.
4. **Empathy:** Understanding and sharing the feelings of others.
5. **Social Skills:** Building and maintaining healthy relationships.

For instance, a founder who notices a team member's waning enthusiasm and addresses it with empathy and encouragement fosters a supportive work environment. This not only boosts morale but also enhances productivity.

Personal Anecdote: Learning to Lead with Empathy

In one of my early ventures, I struggled with high turnover rates among my team. I realized I was so focused on achieving targets that I overlooked the personal struggles of my employees. After implementing regular one-on-one check-ins and genuinely listening to their concerns, the workplace culture improved dramatically, and our retention rates increased by 40%.

2

Building Your Startup Team

In a symphony, the conductor wields the baton to bring harmony to the music. Similarly, as an entrepreneur, your ability to assemble and lead a team will determine your startup's success. The right team can turn an idea into a thriving enterprise, while a mismatched one can derail even the best-laid plans. This chapter focuses on the art of team building—finding, nurturing, and harmonizing the diverse talents that will fuel your startup's growth.

The Power of People: Why Your Team Matters

A startup's success is rarely the result of one person's efforts. It's the synergy of a team that drives innovation, solves complex problems, and scales the business. Consider some of the most successful startups: Steve Jobs had Steve Wozniak at Apple, and Larry Page had Sergey Brin at Google. Their partnerships highlight the importance of complementary skills and shared vision.

Your team will play a crucial role in:

- **Driving Innovation**: Diverse perspectives lead to creative problem-solving.
- **Executing the Vision**: Turning ideas into reality requires a collaborative effort.
- **Building a Culture**: A strong team sets the tone for company values and practices.

Assembling the Right Players

1. Identifying Core Roles

In the early stages, you need a lean but effective team. Prioritize roles that are essential for your business model. For example:

- A **technical lead** for a tech startup.
- A **marketing strategist** for a consumer-focused business.

- A **financial advisor** to manage budgets and funding.

2. Hiring for Potential, Not Just Experience

Early-stage startups thrive on adaptability. While experience is valuable, prioritize candidates who are:

- **Quick Learners**: They can acquire new skills as the startup evolves.
- **Resourceful**: They find creative solutions to challenges.
- **Culturally Aligned**: They resonate with your startup's mission and values.

3. Building a Network

Tap into your network to find team members. Attend industry events, leverage LinkedIn, and connect with alumni groups. Referrals from trusted connections often yield high-quality candidates.

Harmonizing the Team: Creating a Collaborative Culture

1. Establishing Clear Roles and Responsibilities

Ambiguity can lead to conflicts and inefficiencies. From the outset, define:

- **Individual Responsibilities**: Outline who handles what.
- **Collaborative Goals**: Foster teamwork by setting shared objectives.

2. Encouraging Open Communication

A symphony's success depends on every musician hearing each other. Similarly, startups thrive on transparent communication. Foster an environment where:

- Ideas are openly shared.
- Feedback is constructive and actionable.
- Issues are addressed promptly.

3. Leading by Example

As the founder, you set the tone. Demonstrate the values you want your team to embody—whether it's resilience, adaptability, or creativity. Remember, your team looks to you for guidance and inspiration.

Case Study: Airbnb's Founding Trio

Airbnb's journey offers valuable insights into team building. Founders Brian Chesky, Joe Gebbia, and Nathan Blecharczyk brought unique strengths to the table:

- **Brian Chesky** focused on design and branding.
- **Joe Gebbia** specialized in user experience.
- **Nathan Blecharczyk** provided technical expertise.

Their ability to align their skills and maintain a shared vision helped Airbnb evolve from a simple idea to a global platform.

Nurturing Talent: Developing Your Team's Potential

1. Providing Opportunities for Growth

Invest in your team's development through:

- **Training Programs**: Equip them with new skills.
- **Challenging Projects**: Encourage innovation and problem-solving.

- **Mentorship**: Guide them through career development.

2. Recognizing and Rewarding Contributions

Celebrate milestones and individual achievements. Recognition boosts morale and fosters loyalty.

Exercises: Building Your Dream Team

1. **Define Your Ideal Team**: List the key roles and qualities you need in your team. Reflect on how these roles align with your startup's goals.
2. **Team Assessment**: For existing teams, evaluate strengths, weaknesses, and areas for development.
3. **Create a Culture Statement**: Outline the values and behaviors you want to instill in your team. Use this as a guide during hiring and onboarding.

Reflection Questions

1. What skills and traits are most critical for your team at this stage of your startup?

2. How can you ensure that your team members feel valued and motivated?
3. What steps can you take to address any current gaps in your team?

Building a startup team is like assembling an orchestra. Each member must master their part while working in harmony with others. As the conductor, your role is to bring out the best in your team, ensuring that every note contributes to the melody of success. In the next chapter, we'll delve into creating a product or service that resonates with your target audience, completing the foundation for your startup symphony.

3

Crafting Your Product or Service

If a startup is a symphony, then the product or service you offer is its melody—the element that captivates your audience and keeps them coming back for more. This chapter explores the art and science of creating a product or service that not only meets your customers' needs but also resonates deeply with their aspirations and values.

Identifying Your Target Audience

Before creating a compelling melody, you must understand who you are playing for. Your target audience forms the core of your business. Start by developing detailed customer personas that reflect demographics, preferences, pain points, and behaviors. Segment your market based on shared characteristics, such as age, location, or buying habits, and validate these assumptions through surveys, interviews, and focus groups to ensure alignment with reality.

Addressing Pain Points

A great product solves a problem or fulfills a need. Observe your audience to study their behavior and identify gaps in existing solutions. Ask relevant questions to uncover challenges they face and their current approaches to addressing these issues. Finally, prioritize solutions that are urgent, pervasive, and underserved.

The Iterative Process: Designing a Winning Product

Prototyping and Testing

Creating a product is an iterative process. Start with a Minimum Viable Product (MVP)—a basic version that addresses the core problem—to test market demand, gather user feedback, and minimize initial investment. Engage your target audience in testing, provide channels for feedback, and use these insights for continuous improvement.

Balancing Features and Focus

While it's tempting to pack your product with features, simplicity often yields better results.

Prioritize core functionalities that deliver the most value, avoid non-essential additions that dilute impact, and ensure the product remains intuitive and user-friendly.

Differentiation: Standing Out in a Crowded Market

Finding Your Unique Value Proposition (UVP)

Your UVP sets your product apart. Define what makes you different by focusing on aspects competitors don't offer. Communicate this value clearly through simple and customer-focused messaging, and validate its resonance with your target audience.

Branding and Storytelling

The story behind your product can be as powerful as the product itself. Craft a narrative that emotionally connects with your audience, aligns with your startup's mission, and highlights the impact your product can have. Effective storytelling ensures your product remains memorable.

Case Study: Dropbox's Simple Yet Powerful Start

When Dropbox launched, it concentrated on one key feature: seamless file sharing and storage. By addressing a widespread pain point—managing files across devices—Dropbox quickly gained traction. Its emphasis on simplicity and usability became its hallmark, proving that a focused product can create massive impact.

Exercises: Crafting Your Product or Service

To refine your approach to product development:

1. Create a customer persona by detailing your ideal customer's needs, challenges, and goals.
2. Map the customer journey to outline interactions with your product, from discovery to purchase and beyond.
3. Refine your MVP by identifying core features and planning iterative improvements.

Reflection Questions

As you develop your product, consider:

1. What problem does your product solve, and how does it improve your customers' lives?

2. How do you differentiate your product from competitors?
3. What steps can you take to gather feedback and continuously refine your product?

The melody of a symphony draws listeners in and keeps them engaged. Similarly, your product or service should captivate your audience, addressing their needs while delivering a memorable experience. In the next chapter, we'll explore strategies for bringing your melody to the masses—marketing and launching your startup successfully.

4

Marketing and Launching Your Startup

The most exquisite symphony is incomplete without an audience to appreciate its beauty. Similarly, the most innovative product or service can fall short if it doesn't reach the right audience. This chapter explores how to amplify your startup's impact through effective marketing and a well-orchestrated launch.

Building the Buzz: Crafting a Marketing Strategy

Understanding Your Audience

Marketing starts with knowing your audience. Leverage the customer personas you created in earlier chapters to design targeted campaigns. Ask yourself:

- Where does your audience spend time online and offline?

- What messages resonate with their needs and aspirations?
- How do they make purchasing decisions?

Creating a Unique Brand Voice

Your brand is the personality of your startup. Develop a voice that reflects your values and resonates with your audience. Whether your tone is playful, professional, or inspirational, consistency is key. A strong brand identity builds trust and recognition over time.

Leveraging Digital Channels

In today's digital-first world, online channels are crucial for marketing your startup. Focus on:

- **Social Media**: Engage your audience on platforms like Instagram, LinkedIn, or TikTok. Share stories, updates, and customer testimonials.
- **Content Marketing**: Create blogs, videos, and infographics that provide value and establish your expertise.
- **Email Campaigns**: Build an email list and maintain regular communication with potential customers.

Traditional Marketing Still Matters

While digital marketing is vital, don't underestimate the power of traditional methods. Depending on your audience, consider:

- Networking events and trade shows.
- Local advertising, such as billboards or flyers.
- Public relations efforts to gain media coverage.

Timing is Everything: Planning Your Launch

A successful product launch is like a crescendo in a symphony, capturing attention and generating excitement. Follow these steps to plan your launch effectively:

Pre-Launch Preparation

1. **Build Anticipation**: Tease your product through sneak peeks, countdowns, or pre-launch signups.
2. **Secure Early Adopters**: Identify influencers, partners, or loyal

customers who can advocate for your product.

3. **Test the Waters**: Conduct a soft launch or beta test to gather feedback and fine-tune your offering.

The Launch Day

1. **Make an Impact**: Use a bold, attention-grabbing campaign to announce your product. Consider a launch event, live stream, or viral social media post.
2. **Engage the Media**: Share press releases and pitch stories to journalists and bloggers.
3. **Incentivize Engagement**: Offer discounts, free trials, or exclusive perks to early adopters.

Post-Launch Follow-Up

1. **Monitor Feedback**: Actively collect and respond to customer reviews and suggestions.
2. **Evaluate Metrics**: Measure the success of your launch through KPIs like website traffic, conversion rates, and sales.

3. **Iterate and Improve**: Use the data collected to refine your product and marketing strategies.

Personal Anecdote: Lessons from My First Launch

When I launched my first startup, a book publication house, I was both excited and nervous. We had spent months curating an anthology of emerging authors, believing it would resonate deeply with readers. However, the initial reception was lukewarm. Upon reflection, I realized we had overlooked two critical aspects: truly understanding our target readers and creating buzz before the launch. We went back to the drawing board, reached out to literary communities for feedback, and organized engaging pre-launch events, including book readings and online campaigns. This renewed approach resulted in a surge of interest and sales within weeks of the relaunch. The experience underscored the importance of preparation, audience connection, and adaptability in creating a successful launch.

Case Study: The Tesla Model 3 Launch

Tesla's Model 3 launch in 2016 is a masterclass in marketing and anticipation. By announcing the product years in advance, opening pre-orders with a refundable deposit, and creating a buzz through Elon Musk's social media presence, Tesla generated $14 billion in potential sales within a week. Their strategy combined innovation, exclusivity, and effective communication to amplify their impact.

Exercises: Preparing for Your Launch

1. **Create a Marketing Plan**: Outline the channels, messages, and budget for your campaign.
2. **Plan a Launch Event**: Design a detailed plan for how you will unveil your product.
3. **Define Your Metrics**: Identify the KPIs you will track to evaluate your success.

Reflection Questions

1. What is your startup's unique story, and how can you communicate it effectively?

2. Which marketing channels are most relevant to your audience?
3. How will you maintain momentum after your product launch?

In the symphony of entrepreneurship, marketing and launching your startup are the instruments that ensure your melody is heard far and wide. With a thoughtful strategy and relentless execution, you can amplify your impact and turn your startup into a recognizable brand. In the next chapter, we'll delve into scaling your business and sustaining growth over time.

5

Growing Your Startup Sustainably

Once your startup has launched and gained traction, the next challenge is growth. Scaling a business is like expanding a symphony orchestra—it requires careful coordination, strategic investments, and a focus on sustaining quality as you grow. In this chapter, we explore the principles of scaling your startup while maintaining its core identity.

Assessing Readiness: Knowing When to Scale

Scaling too soon can be as damaging as scaling too late. Here are key indicators that your startup is ready for growth:

- **Strong Market Demand**: Consistently meeting or exceeding sales targets and seeing ongoing customer interest.

- **Operational Stability**: Efficient core processes and a team capable of handling increased workloads without compromising quality.
- **Financial Health**: Adequate cash flow or secured funding to support growth initiatives.
- **Product-Market Fit**: A product or service that customers value and that effectively solves their problems.

However, be wary of common pitfalls such as overexpansion without a solid foundation, neglecting core values, and ignoring customer feedback during the growth process.

Strategies for Sustainable Growth

To scale sustainably, focus on building systems that grow with your business:

- **Technology**: Invest in automation tools, cloud-based platforms, and scalable infrastructure.
- **Processes**: Standardize workflows and ensure documentation is in place to maintain efficiency.
- **Talent**: Hire strategically, aligning roles with long-term goals.

Reaching new audiences is another critical aspect of growth. Consider entering new geographic or demographic markets, forming partnerships with complementary businesses, or incentivizing existing customers to make referrals. Additionally, diversifying revenue streams through upselling, cross-selling, subscription models, or licensing your brand can mitigate risks associated with dependency on a single income source.

Managing Growing Pains

As you scale, maintaining quality and preserving company culture are paramount. Implement rigorous quality assurance processes and foster a culture of excellence within your team. Define and communicate your values clearly, prioritize team-building activities, and hire individuals who align with your mission. Financial discipline is also critical—monitor cash flow closely, avoid unnecessary expenses, and seek professional advice when needed.

Case Study: Airbnb's Global Expansion

Airbnb's journey from a small startup to a global leader in the hospitality industry offers valuable insights into scaling sustainably. The founders focused on operational efficiency and used localized approaches to enter new markets, maintaining their mission of creating unique travel experiences. By leveraging technology and fostering community trust, Airbnb scaled effectively without losing its core identity.

Exercises: Planning for Growth

1. **Scalability Audit**: Evaluate your current operations to identify bottlenecks and opportunities for improvement.
2. **Market Research**: Explore potential new customer segments or geographic markets and analyze their needs.
3. **Growth Roadmap**: Outline specific milestones, resources required, and timelines for scaling your business.

Reflection Questions

1. What steps can you take to ensure your operations are scalable?
2. How will you expand your customer base while maintaining strong relationships with existing customers?
3. What strategies will you use to preserve your company culture during growth?

Scaling is the art of balancing ambition with responsibility. By focusing on sustainable practices and staying true to your mission, you can ensure that your startup's symphony continues to resonate powerfully as it grows. In the next chapter, we'll explore how to navigate challenges and pivot effectively when faced with obstacles, ensuring your symphony continues to thrive.

6

Securing Funding

Demystifying the Funding Landscape Securing funding is one of the most critical and challenging aspects of building a startup. The right funding not only provides the resources you need to grow but also brings validation and credibility to your venture. This chapter explores the various funding options available to startups and how to navigate this complex landscape effectively.

Bootstrapping: Starting with What You Have

Bootstrapping involves using your personal savings or revenue generated from the business to fund your startup. While it requires financial discipline, bootstrapping allows you to retain full ownership and control over your company. For example, Sara, the founder of an online art supplies store, started her business with just $2,000 from her savings. By managing expenses judiciously and reinvesting profits, Sara scaled her business to a million-dollar enterprise within five years.

Angel Investors and Venture Capitalists
Angel investors and venture capitalists (VCs) are common sources of external funding for startups. Angel investors are typically high-net-worth individuals who provide capital in exchange for equity or convertible debt. VCs, on the other hand, are professional investors who manage pooled funds from institutions or wealthy individuals.

When approaching these investors, it's crucial to have a solid business plan and a compelling pitch. Investors want to see a scalable business model, a clear understanding of the market, and a capable team. Prepare for tough questions about your revenue projections, competitive advantage, and exit strategy.

Crowdfunding: Tapping into the Power of the Crowd
Crowdfunding platforms like Kickstarter and Indiegogo have democratized the funding process, enabling entrepreneurs to raise money from a large number of people. Success in crowdfunding requires a well-crafted campaign with a clear value proposition, engaging visuals, and a compelling story.

Highlighting the benefits of your product or service and offering attractive rewards can motivate potential backers.

The Art of the Pitch

Your pitch is your chance to make a lasting impression on potential investors. A compelling pitch is concise, engaging, and backed by data. Start with a powerful opening that captures attention, followed by a clear explanation of the problem you're solving and how your solution stands out. Use visuals like charts and graphs to illustrate key points and practice delivering your pitch confidently.

Case Study: A Winning Pitch

Ankit, the founder of a fitness-tech startup, secured $500,000 in seed funding by delivering a pitch that combined storytelling with data. He began by sharing a personal anecdote about his struggle to stay fit while working a demanding job. Ankit then introduced his product—a wearable device that provided personalized fitness recommendations—and supported his claims with market research and customer testimonials.

Managing Financial Health

Securing funding is just the beginning; managing it wisely is equally important. Create a detailed budget that accounts for operational expenses, marketing, product development, and contingencies. Use financial tools to track cash flow, monitor expenses, and ensure you stay within budget.

Avoiding Common Financial Pitfalls

Many startups fail due to poor financial management. Avoid these common mistakes:

- Overspending on non-essential items.
- Underestimating the importance of a financial buffer.
- Failing to monitor cash flow regularly.

By securing the right funding and managing it effectively, you can build a strong financial foundation for your startup's growth and success.

7

Navigating Challenges and Adapting to Change

In the journey of building a startup, challenges are inevitable. Whether it's market shifts, internal conflicts, or unforeseen external events, the ability to adapt and persevere defines successful entrepreneurs. Sustaining harmony in your symphony requires not just resilience but also a proactive approach to identifying and addressing obstacles. This chapter explores how to navigate challenges effectively and position your startup for long-term success.

Understanding the Nature of Challenges

Challenges often come in different forms, each testing your resolve and ingenuity. Market-related challenges, such as declining demand or increasing competition, can threaten your growth. Internal challenges, like team conflicts or resource constraints, may disrupt operations. External factors, such as economic downturns or regulatory changes, can pose unexpected risks. Recognizing these challenges early and categorizing them helps in crafting appropriate solutions.

One common mistake entrepreneurs make is viewing challenges as purely negative. Instead, reframing them as opportunities for growth can shift your perspective. Challenges often push you to innovate, refine processes, and strengthen your resolve. For instance, an economic downturn might force you to optimize costs and discover more efficient ways of operating, leading to long-term benefits.

Building a Resilient Mindset

Resilience starts with mindset. As a leader, your attitude sets the tone for your team. Cultivating emotional intelligence allows you to stay composed under pressure and make rational decisions. Learning from failures is equally important; every setback contains lessons that can guide future actions.

Consider adopting practices that enhance mental resilience, such as:

- **Reflection:** Take time to analyze challenges objectively. What triggered the issue, and what solutions can be explored? Journaling your thoughts and lessons can provide clarity and perspective over time.

- **Adaptability:** Stay open to changing your approach if initial strategies don't work. Being flexible allows you to explore alternate paths to success rather than fixating on a singular solution.
- **Support Networks:** Lean on mentors, advisors, or peers who have faced similar challenges and can offer guidance. Networking groups and entrepreneurial communities can provide invaluable insights and encouragement.

A strong example of resilience comes from Howard Schultz, the founder of Starbucks. In his early days, he faced rejection from numerous investors when pitching his vision of a coffeehouse culture in America. Instead of giving up, Schultz used the feedback to refine his pitch and persisted, eventually securing the funding he needed. Today, Starbucks is a global brand.

Strategies for Problem-Solving

Effective problem-solving requires a structured approach. First, clearly define the problem. For example, instead of saying "Sales are low," identify specific causes, such as poor lead conversion or ineffective marketing campaigns. Once defined, brainstorm possible solutions, involving your team to leverage diverse perspectives.

Prioritization is key. Not all problems need immediate attention, and focusing on high-impact areas ensures efficient use of resources. Implement solutions in stages, monitoring outcomes and making adjustments as needed.

The Importance of Root Cause Analysis

Many entrepreneurs waste resources addressing symptoms rather than underlying causes. Tools like the "5 Whys" method—asking "Why?" repeatedly to drill down to the root of an issue—can be instrumental in uncovering deeper problems. For instance, if customer complaints about delivery delays arise, digging deeper might reveal inefficiencies in supply chain management rather than mere logistical hiccups.

The Art of Pivoting

Sometimes, challenges reveal deeper issues that necessitate a pivot—a fundamental change in your business model, product, or strategy. Pivoting isn't a sign of failure but a strategic move to align with market realities.

For example, Instagram began as a location-based social network called Burbn. Realizing that users were primarily interested in photo-sharing features, the founders pivoted to focus solely on this aspect, leading to massive success. Similarly, Slack originated as an internal communication tool for a gaming company before its creators pivoted to commercialize it as a standalone product.

When considering a pivot, ask yourself:

- Is the current model unsustainable or misaligned with market demand?
- Do we have the resources and time to execute a pivot effectively?
- Will this change better serve our target audience?

A successful pivot often involves clear communication with stakeholders, including your team, investors, and customers.

Transparency builds trust and ensures that everyone is aligned with the new direction.

Maintaining Team Morale During Tough Times

Challenges can take a toll on your team's morale. Transparent communication is essential during such periods. Share the nature of the challenge, your plans to address it, and how the team can contribute. Involving your team fosters a sense of ownership and motivates them to work toward solutions.

Recognize and celebrate small wins, even during difficult phases. Appreciation boosts morale and reinforces a positive culture. Additionally, provide avenues for team members to voice concerns and suggest ideas. Listening actively and showing empathy can make a significant difference.

Building a resilient team also requires investing in their well-being. Offer resources like professional development programs, mental health support, or flexible work arrangements to help your team cope with stress. A motivated and supported team is better equipped to tackle challenges and drive innovation.

Leveraging Innovation to Overcome Obstacles

Innovation is often born out of necessity. During challenging times, encourage your team to think creatively. Host brainstorming sessions, explore emerging technologies, and challenge assumptions. Even small innovations can create breakthroughs, setting your startup apart from competitors.

For instance, during the COVID-19 pandemic, many restaurants pivoted to online delivery models and introduced innovative menu options to adapt to changing consumer behaviors. These adjustments not only kept them afloat but also opened up new revenue streams for the future.

Case Study: Netflix's Adaptation to Market Changes

Netflix's transition from a DVD rental service to a streaming platform is a prime example of navigating challenges through innovation and adaptability. Facing declining demand for physical rentals, the company recognized the potential of digital streaming early on. By investing heavily in technology and original content, Netflix not only survived but became a global entertainment giant. The lesson here is clear: adapting to change and staying ahead of trends can turn challenges into opportunities.

Exercises: Strengthening Your Resilience

1. **Challenge Mapping:** List the top three challenges your startup faces. For each, identify root causes and potential solutions.
2. **Scenario Planning:** Consider worst-case, best-case, and most-likely scenarios for a major challenge. Develop contingency plans for each.
3. **Innovation Sprint:** Organize a team session focused on generating creative solutions for a pressing issue. Test and implement the most viable ideas.

Reflection Questions

1. How do you typically respond to challenges, and how can you improve your approach?
2. Are there opportunities hidden within your current challenges?
3. What steps can you take to maintain team morale and cohesion during difficult times?

4. How can innovation play a role in overcoming your most pressing obstacles?

Challenges are an inevitable part of any entrepreneurial journey. By viewing them as opportunities for growth, cultivating resilience, and staying adaptable, you can navigate even the most turbulent times. The key is to remain focused on your mission while embracing the changes that lead to a stronger, more harmonious startup. In the next chapter, we'll explore strategies for fostering long-term partnerships and collaborations to solidify your startup's place in the market.

8

Fostering Partnerships and Collaborations

Success in the entrepreneurial world isn't achieved in isolation. The most successful startups leverage partnerships and collaborations to extend their reach, enhance their capabilities, and build lasting value. In this chapter, we will explore the importance of partnerships, how to identify the right collaborators, and strategies to cultivate and sustain these relationships for mutual benefit.

The Importance of Partnerships

Partnerships can amplify your startup's potential in several ways. Strategic alliances can open doors to new markets, provide access to resources and expertise, and enhance credibility in the eyes of customers and investors. Consider companies like Spotify and Uber, which partnered to allow riders to customize their in-car music experience. Such collaborations create unique customer experiences that wouldn't be possible otherwise.

Beyond customer-facing partnerships, collaborations can streamline operations. Partnering with suppliers, technology providers, or logistics companies can significantly improve efficiency and reduce costs. For example, many e-commerce startups partner with fulfillment services to ensure smooth operations without investing heavily in infrastructure.

Identifying the Right Partners

Not all partnerships are created equal. The success of a collaboration depends on finding the right fit. Start by asking these questions:

1. **Shared Goals**: Does the potential partner share your vision and objectives? Alignment in goals ensures that both parties benefit from the partnership.

2. **Complementary Strengths**: Does the partner bring something to the table that you lack? For instance, if your startup excels in product innovation but lacks marketing expertise, a

partnership with a marketing agency could be ideal.

3. **Reputation and Reliability**: Is the partner well-regarded in their industry? Associating with a credible partner enhances your brand's reputation, while unreliable partners can tarnish it.
4. **Cultural Fit**: Does the partner's organizational culture align with yours? Differences in work styles or values can lead to conflicts down the line.

Approaching Potential Collaborators

When reaching out to potential partners, it's essential to present a compelling value proposition. What unique benefits can your startup offer them? Clearly articulate how the partnership will create value for both parties. Be prepared to discuss your startup's strengths, market position, and long-term vision.

Building relationships takes time. Start by establishing informal connections through networking events, industry conferences, or online platforms like LinkedIn. Once a rapport is built, move toward formal discussions, emphasizing transparency and trust.

Structuring Partnerships

Successful collaborations are built on clear terms and mutual respect. When formalizing a partnership:

- **Define Roles and Responsibilities**: Clearly outline what each party will contribute and their specific obligations.
- **Set Measurable Goals**: Establish key performance indicators (KPIs) to evaluate the success of the partnership.
- **Draft Legal Agreements**: Protect both parties by formalizing the partnership in writing. Include clauses for conflict resolution, intellectual property rights, and termination terms.

It's also essential to schedule regular check-ins to evaluate progress and address any concerns. Open communication ensures the partnership remains aligned with its objectives.

Overcoming Challenges in Collaborations

While partnerships can be incredibly rewarding, they come with their own set of challenges. Misaligned expectations, communication breakdowns, or shifting priorities can strain relationships. To navigate these hurdles:

- **Address Issues Early**: Don't let small misunderstandings escalate. Open dialogue can resolve most conflicts.
- **Be Flexible**: Circumstances change, and partnerships must adapt. Be willing to revisit terms and adjust as needed.
- **Maintain Mutual Respect**: Even in disagreements, prioritize respect and professionalism to preserve the relationship.

Case Study: Apple and Nike's Collaboration

Apple and Nike's partnership in creating the Nike+iPod Sports Kit exemplifies the power of collaboration. By combining Apple's technological expertise with Nike's deep understanding of athletes, the two companies created a product that revolutionized fitness tracking. Their shared vision of enhancing athletic performance through technology made this partnership a resounding success.

Exercises: Building Partnerships

1. **Partner Mapping**: Identify potential collaborators in your industry. List their strengths, goals, and how a partnership could benefit both parties.
2. **Value Proposition Development**: Craft a pitch highlighting what your startup brings to a potential partnership. Focus on mutual benefits.
3. **Collaboration Audit**: Review existing partnerships. Are they meeting expectations? Identify areas for improvement or potential new opportunities.

Reflection Questions

1. What gaps in your startup could be filled through partnerships?
2. How can you ensure that potential collaborations align with your values and vision?
3. What steps can you take to build and sustain trust with partners?

Collaborations and partnerships are the bridges that connect your startup to new opportunities and resources. By cultivating meaningful relationships, you can amplify your impact and create a foundation for sustainable growth. In the next chapter, we'll delve into how technology and emerging trends can be leveraged to keep your startup at the forefront of innovation.

9

Embracing Technology and Trends

In today's fast-evolving business landscape, staying ahead of technological advancements and market trends is not just an option—it's a necessity. The startups that thrive are those that embrace innovation and use it as a springboard to redefine possibilities. In this chapter, we'll explore the role of technology and trends in shaping your startup's future, how to identify relevant advancements, and strategies for integrating them effectively.

The Role of Technology in Startups

Technology serves as the backbone of most modern startups. From streamlining operations to improving customer engagement, the right tools can significantly enhance efficiency and scalability. Consider the transformative impact of cloud computing, artificial intelligence, and blockchain on various industries. For example, AI-driven tools can automate customer support, while blockchain ensures secure transactions for fintech startups.

Startups must view technology not merely as a support function but as a core enabler. For instance, companies like Zoom leveraged video conferencing technology to redefine remote work dynamics, becoming indispensable during the pandemic. Recognizing the potential of emerging technologies can position your startup as a disruptor rather than a follower.

Identifying Relevant Trends

With countless technological trends emerging, determining which ones align with your business is critical. Here are steps to identify and evaluate trends:

- **Industry Analysis**: Monitor industry reports, research papers, and market analysis to identify emerging technologies relevant to your sector.
- **Competitor Benchmarking**: Study how competitors are adopting new technologies and assess their success.
- **Customer Feedback**: Engage with your customers to understand their

evolving needs and preferences, which may indicate shifts in market demand.

- **Tech Forums and Events**: Participate in conferences, webinars, and hackathons to stay informed about cutting-edge advancements.

Once identified, analyze the feasibility of integrating these technologies into your operations. Factors such as cost, scalability, and alignment with your startup's mission should guide your decisions.

Integrating Technology into Your Startup

Adopting new technologies can be daunting, especially for resource-constrained startups. Here's a structured approach to ensure seamless integration:

1. **Start Small**: Begin with pilot projects to test the technology's effectiveness before scaling up.

2. **Collaborate with Experts**: Partner with tech consultants or hire specialists to guide implementation.

3. **Train Your Team**: Ensure your workforce is equipped to leverage new tools effectively. Regular training

sessions and workshops can help bridge skill gaps.

4. **Measure Impact**: Use metrics to evaluate the technology's contribution to your goals. For instance, if you've implemented an AI chatbot, track metrics like response time and customer satisfaction.

Balancing Innovation with Practicality

While embracing innovation is crucial, it's equally important to avoid "shiny object syndrome"—chasing every new trend without a clear strategy. Focus on technologies that solve specific problems or enhance value for your customers. For instance, if your startup operates in logistics, investing in IoT sensors to monitor shipments might yield better results than adopting virtual reality tools.

Regularly revisit your tech stack to ensure it remains relevant and efficient. Outdated systems can become liabilities, so periodic upgrades and migrations are essential.

Emerging Trends to Watch

Several trends are poised to reshape the startup ecosystem in the coming years. Some of the most promising include:

- **Artificial Intelligence and Machine Learning**: Automating decision-making processes, enhancing customer experiences, and personalizing offerings.
- **Blockchain Technology**: Revolutionizing industries like finance, supply chain, and healthcare with secure, transparent, and tamper-proof systems.
- **Green Technology**: Innovations focused on sustainability, such as renewable energy solutions and eco-friendly materials.
- **5G Connectivity**: Enabling faster, more reliable communication, particularly for IoT-driven businesses.
- **Augmented and Virtual Reality**: Transforming user experiences in gaming, education, and e-commerce.

Staying informed about these trends ensures your startup remains competitive and future-ready.

Case Study: Tesla's Technological Edge

Tesla exemplifies how leveraging technology can disrupt an industry. By integrating advanced battery technologies, autonomous driving software, and over-the-air updates, Tesla redefined the automobile industry. Their focus on innovation didn't just create electric vehicles; it set new benchmarks for sustainability and smart technology integration. Startups can learn from Tesla's commitment to pushing technological boundaries while remaining customer-centric.

Exercises: Staying Ahead in Technology

1. **Tech Roadmap**: Develop a roadmap for adopting new technologies over the next 2-5 years. Identify priorities, potential costs, and expected benefits.
2. **Trend Analysis**: Choose one emerging trend relevant to your industry and research its potential impact. Present findings to your team.
3. **Skill Assessment**: Evaluate your team's current technical skills and identify areas requiring upskilling. Plan training initiatives accordingly.

Reflection Questions

1. How does technology currently support your startup's operations and goals?
2. Which emerging technologies or trends excite you most, and how can they enhance your offerings?
3. What steps can you take to ensure your team stays adaptable and tech-savvy?

Embracing technology and trends is not just about staying relevant; it's about leading the charge into the future. By strategically adopting advancements and fostering a culture of innovation, your startup can not only survive but thrive in an increasingly competitive world. In the next chapter, we'll explore the critical role of financial management in sustaining and scaling your startup.

10

Building a Legacy Beyond the Startup Stage

In the symphony of entrepreneurship, the most powerful movements are often reserved for the encore. This is the moment when a performance goes beyond expectations, leaving an indelible impression on the audience. Similarly, for startups, the post-success phase is not just about sustaining operations but about creating a legacy that resonates for years to come. This chapter explores how entrepreneurs can transition from initial success to enduring impact, building organizations that stand the test of time.

Sustaining Momentum

Achieving success as a startup is a remarkable feat, but sustaining it is an entirely different challenge. As markets evolve and competitors emerge, startups must continuously adapt to maintain relevance and growth.

Evolving Product Lines and Services

One key to longevity is innovation. Businesses must revisit their product or service offerings regularly to ensure they remain relevant to customer needs. For example, consider how Amazon evolved from an online bookstore to a global e-commerce powerhouse, leveraging customer data to expand into cloud computing, streaming, and more.

To avoid stagnation:

- **Invest in Research and Development (R&D):** Allocate resources to explore new technologies and trends.
- **Listen to Your Customers:** Use feedback to guide improvements and new offerings.
- **Experiment Responsibly:** Test new ideas on a small scale before committing significant resources.

Continuous Customer Engagement

Customer loyalty is the lifeblood of any long-lasting business. Maintaining a strong connection with your audience requires:

- **Personalized Experiences:** Leverage data to tailor interactions and offers.
- **Transparency:** Build trust by being honest about your practices, successes, and even challenges.
- **Loyalty Programs:** Incentivize repeat business through rewards and exclusive benefits.

The Power of a Strong Culture

As startups grow, preserving a cohesive culture becomes increasingly important. A strong organizational culture not only drives performance but also attracts and retains top talent.

Building Core Values

Core values act as the guiding principles for decision-making and behavior. Successful companies like Patagonia and Zappos emphasize values such as environmental stewardship and exceptional customer service, ensuring alignment across all levels of the organization.

Encouraging Intrapreneurship

Empowering employees to think and act like entrepreneurs fosters innovation. This can be achieved by:

- Offering opportunities for employees to lead projects.
- Creating a culture that rewards creativity and risk-taking.
- Providing platforms for employees to pitch ideas and collaborate on initiatives.

Sustainable Practices for Longevity

In today's business environment, stakeholders increasingly value sustainability. Startups must balance profitability with social and environmental responsibility to build a reputation that resonates with customers and partners.

Embracing ESG Principles

Adopting Environmental, Social, and Governance (ESG) principles demonstrates a commitment to ethical practices. This might include:

- Reducing carbon footprints by optimizing supply chains.
- Ensuring fair labor practices.
- Practicing transparent governance to build stakeholder trust.

Balancing Growth with Responsibility

While rapid growth is often celebrated, unchecked expansion can lead to challenges such as resource depletion and public scrutiny. Sustainable growth involves:

- Scaling at a pace that aligns with organizational capacity.
- Reinforcing ethical practices at every stage of expansion.
- Partnering with like-minded organizations to amplify impact.

Expanding the Vision

Long-term success often requires venturing into new markets and diversifying offerings. However, expansion should never come at the cost of losing sight of your startup's core identity.

Diversifying Revenue Streams

Exploring complementary revenue streams can mitigate risks associated with relying on a single source of income. Examples include:

- Adding subscription models or licensing agreements.
- Offering premium versions of products or services.

- Entering strategic partnerships to co-develop offerings.

Exploring New Markets

When entering new geographic or demographic markets, startups must:

- Conduct thorough market research to understand local needs.
- Adapt products and marketing strategies to align with cultural nuances.
- Build partnerships with local businesses to ease the transition.

Giving Back: Startups with a Purpose

A legacy isn't built solely on profits; it's also about the impact a business makes on society. Startups that prioritize giving back inspire loyalty and foster goodwill.

The Importance of Corporate Social Responsibility (CSR)

CSR initiatives enhance brand reputation and contribute to societal well-being. Examples include:

- Hosting community events or fundraisers.
- Supporting education or environmental programs.
- Donating a portion of profits to charitable causes.

Case Study: TOMS Shoes

TOMS Shoes revolutionized corporate philanthropy with its “One for One” model—for every pair of shoes sold, a pair is donated to someone in need. This simple yet impactful idea not only generated goodwill but also differentiated TOMS in a crowded market.

Legacy Leadership

Creating a lasting legacy requires preparing for the future. Entrepreneurs must develop the next generation of leaders who can carry the torch forward.

Developing Future Leaders

Mentorship and professional development are critical for grooming leadership talent. Strategies include:

- **Leadership Training Programs:** Equip employees with skills to take on higher responsibilities.

- **Shadowing Opportunities:** Allow potential leaders to observe and learn from senior management.
- **Cross-Functional Roles:** Expose team members to different aspects of the business.

Crafting a Succession Plan

A well-thought-out succession plan ensures business continuity. Key components include:

- Identifying and training successors early.
- Establishing clear timelines and transition processes.
- Communicating plans transparently with stakeholders.

Reflection and Exercises

To apply the principles discussed in this chapter, consider the following:

Exercises

1. **Legacy Vision Statement:** Write a vision statement describing the legacy you want your startup to leave.

2. **Culture Audit:** Assess your current organizational culture. Identify strengths and areas for improvement.
3. **Sustainability Roadmap:** Develop a plan to integrate ESG principles into your operations.

Reflection Questions

- How can your startup evolve while staying true to its core mission?
- What steps can you take to ensure your business practices are sustainable?
- How will you prepare future leaders to carry on your vision?

In the symphony of entrepreneurship, the encore is where the performance transcends into something unforgettable. By focusing on sustainability, innovation, and legacy-building, startups can ensure their melodies resonate far beyond their initial success. The journey doesn't end with applause—it begins anew with every note of the encore.

11

Strengthening Partnerships for Enduring Success

Startups thrive not in isolation but through a dynamic interplay with external partners, stakeholders, and communities. Much like a symphony relies on the cohesion of its orchestra, a business relies on partnerships to amplify its strengths and reach new heights. This chapter focuses on the art of cultivating, nurturing, and maximizing partnerships to sustain long-term growth and innovation.

The Role of Partnerships in Scaling a Startup

No startup can achieve enduring success without collaboration. Strategic partnerships allow businesses to:

- **Access Resources and Expertise:** Leverage the strengths of others to complement your capabilities.
- **Enhance Market Reach:** Enter new territories and demographics with the support of established networks.
- **Boost Credibility:** Association with trusted partners lends legitimacy and increases customer confidence.

Types of Strategic Partnerships

1. **Technology Alliances:** Collaborations with tech companies to improve operational efficiency or enhance product offerings.
    - Example: Spotify's integration with social media platforms for seamless music sharing.
2. **Supply Chain Partnerships:** Working with logistics providers to ensure timely deliveries and optimize operations.
    - Example: E-commerce companies partnering with third-party logistics firms for faster last-mile delivery.

3. **Co-Marketing Initiatives:** Joint campaigns with complementary brands to share audiences and reduce marketing costs.
    - Example: A fitness equipment company collaborating with a health app to promote wellness.
4. **Corporate Social Responsibility (CSR) Partnerships:** Aligning with NGOs or community programs to contribute to social causes.
    - Example: Starbucks working with local farmers to ensure sustainable coffee sourcing.

Building Effective Partnerships

Successful partnerships require careful planning and execution. Follow these steps to create alliances that work:

1. Identifying the Right Partners

Begin by defining what you hope to achieve through the partnership. Once clear, evaluate potential partners based on:

- **Alignment of Values:** Do they share your vision and ethical standards?

- **Complementary Strengths:** Do their capabilities fill gaps in your own business?
- **Reputation and Reliability:** Are they well-regarded in the industry and dependable?

2. Establishing Mutually Beneficial Goals

A successful partnership is one where both parties benefit. Outline:

- **Shared Objectives:** Define measurable outcomes that align with both partners' goals.
- **Roles and Responsibilities:** Clearly delineate what each party will contribute.

3. Drafting Formal Agreements

Put the partnership's terms into a written agreement that covers:

- Deliverables and timelines.
- Intellectual property rights.
- Conflict resolution mechanisms.
- Metrics for success evaluation.

4. Communicating Effectively

Regular and transparent communication is essential to sustaining a healthy partnership. Use tools like:

- Scheduled check-ins to assess progress.
- Shared project management platforms for real-time updates.
- Open channels for addressing issues promptly.

Nurturing Long-Term Relationships

Partnerships, like any relationship, require ongoing effort. Invest in building trust and collaboration over time by:

Recognizing Contributions

Acknowledging the efforts and successes of your partners strengthens bonds. Public recognition, shared press releases, or even simple thank-you notes can go a long way.

Adapting to Change

Business environments are dynamic. Partnerships that adapt to evolving circumstances—whether it's shifting market demands or emerging technologies—are more likely to endure.

Measuring Success

Use key performance indicators (KPIs) to evaluate the effectiveness of your partnerships. Examples include:

- Revenue growth attributable to the partnership.
- Customer acquisition or retention rates.
- Operational efficiencies gained.

Case Studies: Partnerships that Transformed Startups

Airbnb and Professional Photographers

To improve the appeal of its listings, Airbnb partnered with professional photographers to provide high-quality visuals. This collaboration enhanced the user experience and contributed to the platform's exponential growth.

Apple and Nike

The collaboration between Apple and Nike on the Nike+iPod Sports Kit brought together cutting-edge technology and sports expertise. This partnership not only expanded Apple's product ecosystem but also solidified Nike's position as an innovator in athletic wear.

The Role of Partnerships in Innovation

Innovation thrives on diversity. By collaborating with external organizations, startups can:

- **Gain Fresh Perspectives:** Exposure to different industries and viewpoints fosters creativity.
- **Accelerate Product Development:** Sharing resources reduces time-to-market.
- **De-Risk Exploration:** Partnerships allow startups to experiment with new ideas without shouldering the entire burden.

Exercises

1. **Partner Mapping:** Identify existing and potential partners for your startup. List how each aligns with your goals and values.
2. **Collaboration Audit:** Evaluate your current partnerships. Are they meeting

their objectives? What could be improved?

3. **Goal Alignment Workshop:** Host a session with a key partner to ensure mutual understanding of goals and expectations.

Reflection Questions

- How do partnerships currently support your business objectives?
- What gaps in your operations could be filled through collaboration?
- How can you ensure your partnerships remain adaptable and resilient?

In the symphony of business, partnerships play a vital role in creating harmony and amplifying impact. By thoughtfully cultivating these relationships, startups can not only scale effectively but also foster innovation, resilience, and a lasting legacy.

12

Navigating Challenges in the Startup Journey

In the unpredictable landscape of entrepreneurship, challenges are inevitable. How a startup anticipates, addresses, and learns from these obstacles often determines its longevity and success. Much like a symphony must adapt to unexpected disruptions without losing its rhythm, a business must remain resilient in the face of adversity. This chapter explores the strategies and mindset required to navigate challenges and emerge stronger.

Understanding the Nature of Challenges

Challenges come in various forms, and their impact can range from minor disruptions to existential threats. Common types include:

- **Market Shifts:** Changes in consumer behavior, emerging competitors, or economic downturns.
- **Operational Hurdles:** Supply chain disruptions, talent shortages, or inefficiencies in internal processes.
- **Financial Strains:** Cash flow issues, funding delays, or unexpected expenses.
- **External Crises:** Natural disasters, regulatory changes, or geopolitical events.

The Opportunity Within Challenges

While challenges can be daunting, they often present opportunities for growth and innovation. Companies that approach obstacles as learning experiences are better equipped to adapt and thrive.

Case Example: Netflix's Transformation

When DVD rentals began to decline, Netflix faced a pivotal challenge. By embracing streaming technology early and investing in original content, the company not only survived but became a global entertainment leader.

Cultivating a Resilient Mindset

Resilience begins with mindset. Entrepreneurs and their teams must adopt a proactive and adaptable approach to challenges.

Key Traits of Resilient Leaders

1. **Emotional Intelligence:** Recognizing and managing emotions to maintain focus under pressure.
2. **Optimism:** Viewing challenges as opportunities rather than setbacks.
3. **Decisiveness:** Making timely and informed decisions, even with incomplete information.
4. **Adaptability:** Being open to change and ready to pivot when necessary.

Building Team Resilience

Encouraging resilience at an organizational level requires:

- **Transparent Communication:** Keeping teams informed fosters trust and collective problem-solving.

- **Continuous Learning:** Offering training programs and workshops to build new skills.
- **Support Systems:** Providing mental health resources and encouraging work-life balance.

Strategies for Problem-Solving

When facing a challenge, structured problem-solving can lead to effective solutions. Consider these steps:

1. Identify the Root Cause

Superficial solutions rarely address the underlying problem. Use tools like the "5 Whys" method to uncover the core issue.

2. Prioritize Actions

Focus on high-impact solutions that address the most critical aspects of the challenge.

3. Engage Stakeholders

Involve team members, advisors, or partners who can offer diverse perspectives and expertise.

4. Implement and Monitor

Execute solutions systematically, and track their effectiveness using key performance indicators (KPIs).

Example: Tesla's Supply Chain Innovations

Facing production delays, Tesla restructured its supply chain, vertically integrating key components. This approach reduced dependency on third parties and improved efficiency.

The Art of Pivoting

Sometimes, the best way to address a challenge is to change direction entirely. Pivoting involves redefining your business model, product, or strategy to better align with market demands.

When to Pivot

- Persistent lack of product-market fit.
- Declining sales or engagement.
- Emerging opportunities in adjacent markets.

How to Pivot Successfully

1. **Analyze Data:** Use customer feedback and performance metrics to guide your decisions.
2. **Communicate Clearly:** Keep stakeholders informed and aligned with the new direction.
3. **Test and Validate:** Pilot the pivot before committing significant resources.

Case Study: Slack's Evolution

Originally developed as a gaming company's internal communication tool, Slack pivoted to become a standalone platform. This shift resulted in its success as a leading collaboration software.

Managing Crises Effectively

Crises demand swift and decisive action. A well-prepared crisis management plan can mitigate damage and maintain stakeholder confidence.

Components of a Crisis Management Plan

1. **Risk Assessment:** Identify potential risks and their likelihood.

2. **Response Framework:** Define roles and responsibilities during a crisis.
3. **Communication Protocols:** Establish clear channels for internal and external communication.
4. **Post-Crisis Evaluation:** Review the response to improve future preparedness.

Example: Johnson & Johnson's Tylenol Recall

In response to a tampering crisis, Johnson & Johnson prioritized customer safety, recalling products and introducing tamper-proof packaging. Their transparent and proactive approach restored public trust.

Leveraging Innovation During Challenges

Innovation often emerges from necessity. During challenging times, encourage creative problem-solving and experimentation.

- **Host Innovation Sprints:** Facilitate brainstorming sessions focused on addressing specific challenges.
- **Invest in Technology:** Explore tools and platforms that can enhance efficiency and adaptability.

- **Collaborate with Partners:** Leverage external expertise and resources for innovative solutions.

Example: Restaurants and COVID-19

Faced with lockdowns, many restaurants adopted online ordering and delivery systems, creating new revenue streams and ensuring survival.

Exercises

1. **Challenge Mapping:** List three significant challenges your startup has faced. Analyze their root causes and outcomes.
2. **Resilience Audit:** Assess your personal and organizational resilience. Identify areas for improvement.
3. **Scenario Planning:** Develop contingency plans for potential future challenges.

Reflection Questions

- How does your startup currently handle challenges, and what can be improved?
- What lessons have past challenges taught you about resilience?

- How can you foster a culture of adaptability and innovation within your team?

Resilience is the cornerstone of enduring success in the startup world. By embracing challenges as opportunities for growth, adopting a proactive mindset, and fostering innovation, startups can not only weather storms but also emerge stronger and more prepared for the future.

13

Building a Data-Driven Organization

In the modern business landscape, data is often described as the new oil—a resource with immense potential when effectively harnessed. For startups, building a data-driven organization is not just a competitive advantage; it's a necessity for long-term success. This chapter explores the principles, tools, and strategies needed to embed data-driven decision-making at the core of your organization.

The Value of a Data-Driven Approach

Organizations that prioritize data are better equipped to:

- **Make Informed Decisions:** Base strategies on actionable insights rather than intuition.

- **Understand Customers:** Gain deeper insights into customer behavior, preferences, and pain points.
- **Optimize Operations:** Identify inefficiencies and implement process improvements.
- **Predict Trends:** Stay ahead by analyzing patterns and forecasting market shifts.

Case Study: Amazon's Data-Centric Growth

Amazon leverages data extensively to optimize inventory, personalize recommendations, and predict customer needs. This relentless focus on data has played a pivotal role in making Amazon a global leader.

Laying the Foundation for a Data-Driven Culture

Becoming a data-driven organization begins with creating the right culture. This involves:

1. Promoting Data Literacy

Equip your team with the skills to understand and utilize data effectively. Strategies include:

- Offering training programs in analytics tools and techniques.
- Encouraging data-driven discussions in meetings.
- Providing resources for continuous learning, such as online courses or workshops.

2. Leadership Commitment

Leadership must model data-driven behavior by:

- Using data to justify decisions.
- Encouraging transparency in how data is collected and used.
- Celebrating successes achieved through data insights.

3. Establishing Data Governance

Clear policies around data management are essential for consistency and security. This includes:

- Defining roles and responsibilities for data access and usage.
- Ensuring compliance with data protection regulations, such as GDPR or CCPA.

- Regularly auditing data practices to maintain integrity.

Building the Right Infrastructure

A robust data infrastructure is crucial for collecting, storing, and analyzing information effectively.

1. Centralized Data Repositories

Implement systems like data warehouses or lakes to consolidate information from various sources. This ensures easy access and reduces silos.

2. Analytics Tools

Equip your organization with tools to analyze and visualize data. Popular options include:

- **Business Intelligence (BI) Tools:** Tableau, Power BI, or Looker.
- **Data Analytics Platforms:** Google Analytics, Mixpanel, or Snowflake.
- **Machine Learning Frameworks:** TensorFlow, PyTorch, or H2O.ai.

3. Scalable Infrastructure

Invest in cloud solutions that grow with your business, such as AWS, Azure, or Google Cloud Platform, to handle increasing data volumes.

4. Real-Time Data Access

Enable real-time analytics to respond quickly to emerging trends or issues. For example, monitoring customer activity during a product launch can provide instant insights for adjustments.

Integrating Data Across Functions

To maximize the value of data, integrate it into every aspect of your operations:

1. Marketing

- Use analytics to measure campaign performance and refine strategies.
- Employ segmentation to target specific customer groups more effectively.

2. Sales

- Analyze conversion rates to identify successful tactics.

- Use predictive analytics to forecast sales and allocate resources efficiently.

3. Operations

- Monitor key performance indicators (KPIs) to identify bottlenecks.
- Optimize supply chain logistics using data insights.

4. Product Development

- Gather user feedback and usage data to inform iterative improvements.
- Test new features through A/B testing to determine effectiveness.

Example: Netflix's Personalization Engine

Netflix uses sophisticated algorithms to analyze viewing habits and recommend content. This data-driven personalization has been key to their customer retention and satisfaction.

Overcoming Challenges in Becoming Data-Driven

Transitioning to a data-driven model isn't without its hurdles. Common challenges include:

1. Data Silos

When information is scattered across departments, it hinders decision-making. Address this by:

- Implementing unified data platforms.
- Encouraging interdepartmental collaboration.

2. Resistance to Change

Some team members may hesitate to adopt new data practices. Overcome this by:

- Highlighting the benefits of data-driven decisions.
- Providing support and training to ease the transition.

3. Ensuring Data Quality

Decisions are only as good as the data behind them. Maintain quality by:

- Regularly cleaning and validating data.
- Setting standards for data entry and management.

4. Balancing Privacy and Personalization

While data provides valuable insights, it's essential to respect customer privacy. Achieve this by:

- Being transparent about data usage.
- Allowing customers to control their data through opt-ins and preferences.

Exercises

1. **Data Inventory Audit:** List all the data sources your startup currently uses. Identify gaps or redundancies.
2. **Dashboard Design:** Create a simple dashboard for tracking a key business metric, such as sales or customer acquisition.
3. **Scenario Analysis:** Use historical data to predict the outcome of a strategic decision, such as launching a new product.

Reflection Questions

- How is data currently used in decision-making within your startup?

- What steps can you take to improve data accessibility and quality?
- How can you balance data-driven strategies with creativity and intuition?

Becoming a data-driven organization is a journey, not a destination. By fostering a culture that values insights, investing in the right tools and infrastructure, and integrating data into every function, startups can unlock new levels of efficiency, innovation, and success. The key is to approach data not as an end but as a means to make smarter, more impactful decisions.

14

Navigating Regulatory Obligations for Startups

Startups often focus on innovation, growth, and scaling, but overlooking compliance can lead to significant penalties and operational setbacks. Adhering to legal and regulatory requirements is not just about avoiding fines; it's about building a strong foundation of trust and credibility. This chapter will guide you through the essentials of corporate compliance, including mandatory filings, key timelines, and best practices to stay on top of your obligations.

The Importance of Compliance

Compliance ensures that your startup operates within the legal framework set by governing authorities. Benefits include:

- **Avoiding Penalties:** Non-compliance can result in hefty fines, legal battles, and reputational damage.
- **Building Credibility:** Adherence to regulations fosters trust among investors, customers, and partners.
- **Facilitating Growth:** A compliant organization is better positioned to scale and attract funding.

Example: In 2019, a high-profile startup faced massive penalties for failing to comply with data protection laws, leading to a loss of customer trust and market share.

Key Areas of Compliance

1. Annual General Meetings (AGMs)

AGMs are a statutory requirement for many companies. They ensure transparency and provide shareholders with a platform to discuss the company's performance.

Checklist for AGMs:

- Schedule the meeting within the prescribed timeline (e.g., within six months of the financial year-end).

- Share the agenda, financial statements, and other relevant documents with shareholders in advance.
- Document the minutes and resolutions passed during the meeting.

2. Financial Filings

Accurate and timely financial reporting is essential for compliance. Key filings include:

- **Annual Financial Statements:** Submit audited financial reports to regulatory bodies.
- **Tax Returns:** File income tax, GST, and other applicable taxes within deadlines.
- **Board Resolutions:** Record and file major decisions made by the board of directors.

3. Employee Compliance

Ensure compliance with labor laws, such as:

- Provident fund and employee insurance contributions.
- Adherence to workplace safety and anti-harassment regulations.

- Issuing offer letters, contracts, and payslips as required by law.

4. Industry-Specific Regulations

Certain industries, such as fintech, healthcare, and e-commerce, have additional compliance requirements. For example:

- **Fintech:** Adhering to anti-money laundering (AML) and know-your-customer (KYC) norms.
- **Healthcare:** Complying with patient data protection and licensing requirements.
- **E-commerce:** Ensuring transparency in pricing, returns, and data usage policies.

5. Environmental, Social, and Governance (ESG) Compliance

As sustainability gains prominence, startups are expected to comply with ESG norms. This includes:

- Reducing environmental impact through sustainable practices.
- Ensuring ethical governance and diversity in leadership.

- Reporting on ESG initiatives in annual reports.

Best Practices for Staying Compliant

1. Create a Compliance Calendar

List all filing deadlines, meetings, and other requirements. Use digital tools to set reminders and track progress.

2. Appoint a Compliance Officer

Designate a team member or hire a specialist to oversee compliance-related activities. Their responsibilities include:

- Monitoring regulatory changes.
- Coordinating with legal and financial advisors.
- Ensuring timely filings and documentation.

3. Leverage Technology

Use compliance management software to automate tasks such as:

- Tracking filing deadlines.
- Generating compliance reports.
- Maintaining records securely.

4. Conduct Regular Audits

Periodic internal audits can help identify gaps and rectify them before they escalate.

5. Educate Your Team

Train employees on relevant regulations, especially those pertaining to their roles. For instance:

- Sales teams should understand data protection laws.
- HR teams should be familiar with labor laws and workplace regulations.

Consequences of Non-Compliance

Failing to comply with regulations can have severe repercussions, including:

- **Financial Penalties:** Fines that can strain resources, especially for startups.
- **Operational Disruptions:** Suspension of licenses or operational activities.
- **Reputational Damage:** Loss of trust among stakeholders.

Example: A well-known ride-sharing company faced backlash and legal action for non-compliance with labor laws, resulting in a significant drop in driver registrations.

Exercises

1. **Compliance Audit:** Review your current compliance status. Identify any gaps and create a plan to address them.
2. **Calendar Creation:** Develop a compliance calendar for your startup, including all key deadlines.
3. **Role Assignment:** Assign compliance responsibilities to team members and outline their tasks.

Reflection Questions

- What are the specific compliance requirements for your industry?
- How can you integrate compliance into your daily operations?
- What steps can you take to ensure your startup stays ahead of regulatory changes?

By prioritizing compliance, startups can avoid unnecessary risks and build a solid foundation for sustainable growth. The key is to view compliance not as a burden but as an integral part of responsible business operations, paving the way for long-term success.

15

Building Connections for Startup Success

Success in the startup world isn't achieved in isolation. Networking—the art of building meaningful relationships—is a critical skill that can open doors to new opportunities, mentorship, funding, and partnerships. This chapter delves into the significance of networking, strategies to expand your circle, and how to leverage connections for long-term growth.

Why Networking Matters

Networking goes beyond exchanging business cards or attending events. It's about cultivating authentic relationships that can:

- **Expand Opportunities:** Introduce you to potential clients, investors, and collaborators.

- **Enhance Knowledge:** Provide insights from experienced professionals and industry leaders.
- **Build Credibility:** Increase your startup's visibility and reputation in the industry.
- **Foster Collaboration:** Enable partnerships that drive innovation and growth.

Example: The founders of PayPal, known as the "PayPal Mafia," leveraged their network to create successful ventures like Tesla, LinkedIn, and YouTube.

Types of Networking

1. Professional Networking

Focuses on connecting with individuals within your industry. Examples include:

- **Industry Conferences:** Attend events relevant to your field to meet peers and experts.
- **Webinars and Online Forums:** Participate in virtual discussions and panels.
- **Professional Organizations:** Join trade groups or associations.

2. Strategic Networking

Target individuals who can directly impact your startup's growth, such as:

- Angel investors and venture capitalists.
- Influential mentors or advisors.
- Decision-makers in key organizations.

3. Community Networking

Involves engaging with your local or online community to:

- Build grassroots support for your startup.
- Find collaborators who share your mission.
- Gain access to hyperlocal opportunities.

Networking Strategies for Startups

1. Prepare Your Elevator Pitch

A concise and compelling elevator pitch is essential. It should:

- Clearly state what your startup does.

- Highlight your unique value proposition.
- Include a call to action, such as scheduling a follow-up meeting.

Example Pitch: "Our startup provides AI-driven analytics tools that help small businesses optimize their operations, saving them time and money. I'd love to discuss how we could bring value to your organization."

2. Leverage Social Media

Platforms like LinkedIn, Twitter, and industry-specific forums are invaluable for building a digital presence. Use them to:

- Share thought leadership content.
- Engage with industry influencers.
- Participate in relevant groups and discussions.

3. Attend Networking Events

Make the most of networking opportunities by:

- Researching attendees in advance and identifying key individuals to connect with.

- Preparing meaningful questions and conversation starters.
- Following up promptly with personalized messages.

4. Offer Value First

Approach networking with a mindset of giving rather than taking. Examples include:

- Sharing resources, insights, or introductions.
- Offering help with challenges your connections face.
- Being a reliable and consistent presence in their professional lives.

5. Build a Personal Advisory Board

Surround yourself with trusted mentors and advisors who can:

- Provide guidance on strategic decisions.
- Offer feedback on challenges.
- Connect you with their networks.

Maintaining Relationships

Building a network is only the first step; maintaining relationships is equally important. Tips include:

- **Regular Check-Ins:** Send occasional emails or messages to stay in touch.
- **Celebrate Milestones:** Congratulate connections on their achievements.
- **Show Gratitude:** Thank individuals for their support or advice.

Overcoming Networking Challenges

1. Overcoming Shyness

For introverts, networking can feel daunting. Strategies to ease anxiety include:

- Practicing your pitch beforehand.
- Starting with smaller, low-pressure events.
- Bringing a colleague or friend for support.

2. Managing Time Constraints

Busy schedules can limit networking opportunities. Overcome this by:

- Scheduling networking into your calendar as a priority.
- Leveraging virtual meetings to save travel time.
- Setting specific goals for each networking activity.

3. Breaking Into New Circles

If you're entering a new industry or market:

- Research key players and organizations.
- Attend events tailored to your new focus.
- Leverage existing contacts for introductions.

Case Studies: Networking Success Stories

1. Airbnb's Funding Journey

Airbnb's founders networked extensively to secure early funding. They participated in startup accelerators, reached out to investors through mutual connections, and refined their pitch based on feedback. These efforts resulted in support from prominent venture capital firms.

2. LinkedIn's Network Effect

LinkedIn itself is a testament to the power of networking. By encouraging professionals to connect, share insights, and collaborate, the platform has become an essential tool for career growth and business development.

Exercises and Reflection

Exercises

1. **Networking Map:** Identify your existing connections and potential opportunities within your network. Highlight key individuals to engage with.
2. **Event Plan:** Research upcoming industry events and create a plan to participate effectively.
3. **Follow-Up System:** Develop a system for tracking and maintaining your connections, such as a CRM tool or a simple spreadsheet.

Reflection Questions

- How can networking contribute to your startup's growth?
- What strategies have worked for you in building connections?

- How can you provide value to your network consistently?

Networking is more than a business activity; it's a lifelong skill that fosters growth, collaboration, and innovation. By building meaningful relationships and maintaining them with care, startups can unlock opportunities that propel them toward success.

16

Creating a Strong Brand Identity

In the crowded marketplace of startups, a strong brand identity is often the distinguishing factor between success and obscurity. A compelling brand goes beyond a logo or a tagline; it tells a story, evokes emotion, and forges a connection with your audience. This chapter explores how to build a brand that resonates, establishes trust, and leaves a lasting impression.

Why Brand Identity Matters

A strong brand identity:

- **Differentiates Your Startup:** Sets you apart from competitors and defines your unique value.
- **Builds Trust and Loyalty:** Encourages customer confidence and long-term relationships.

- **Drives Recognition:** Ensures that your business is memorable and recognizable across touchpoints.
- **Aligns Your Team:** Provides a unified vision and mission for employees to rally behind.

Example: Apple's brand identity—rooted in simplicity, innovation, and premium quality—has cultivated a loyal global following.

Elements of a Strong Brand Identity

1. Vision and Mission

Your vision and mission form the foundation of your brand. They answer fundamental questions:

- **Vision:** What long-term impact do you aspire to make? (e.g., "To connect the world through meaningful experiences.")
- **Mission:** What steps will you take to achieve your vision? (e.g., "Providing seamless video conferencing solutions for global teams.")

2. Core Values

Define the principles that guide your decisions and actions. Examples include:

- Sustainability
- Customer-centricity
- Innovation
- Integrity

3. Target Audience

Understanding your audience allows you to craft a brand that speaks directly to their needs and desires. Create detailed personas that include:

- Demographics (age, gender, income, location).
- Psychographics (values, interests, challenges).
- Buying behavior and preferences.

4. Visual Identity

Your visual elements should be consistent and aligned with your brand's essence:

- **Logo:** A unique, simple design that represents your brand.
- **Color Palette:** Colors that evoke specific emotions or associations.
- **Typography:** Fonts that reflect your tone (e.g., formal, playful, modern).

- **Imagery:** Photos, illustrations, or graphics that reinforce your message.

5. Brand Voice

Your tone and communication style should resonate with your audience. Determine:

- **Tone:** Friendly, authoritative, inspirational, etc.
- **Language:** Formal or conversational.
- **Personality:** How your brand would "sound" in a conversation.

Steps to Build Your Brand Identity

1. Define Your Brand Strategy

Start with a clear strategy that outlines:

- **Positioning:** How do you want your startup to be perceived in the market?
- **Differentiators:** What makes your offering unique?
- **Promise:** What can customers consistently expect from your brand?

2. Conduct Market Research

Understand your competitive landscape and customer expectations. Use tools like surveys, focus groups, and competitor analysis to gather insights.

3. Develop Visual and Verbal Assets

Collaborate with designers and copywriters to create:

- Logos and design templates.
- Taglines, slogans, and key messaging.
- Brand guidelines to ensure consistency across all platforms.

4. Test and Refine

Before launching your brand, test it with a subset of your audience. Gather feedback on:

- Logo and design appeal.
- Messaging clarity and resonance.
- Overall perception of the brand.

5. Launch and Communicate

Introduce your brand to the world through:

- Social media campaigns.
- A dedicated launch event or press release.

- Updated website and marketing materials.

Maintaining Brand Consistency

Consistency is critical to building trust and recognition. Ensure:

- All team members understand and adhere to brand guidelines.
- Messaging remains consistent across platforms, from emails to social media.
- Regular audits to ensure your brand stays relevant and aligned with your mission.

Measuring Brand Success

Track metrics to gauge the effectiveness of your branding efforts, such as:

- **Brand Awareness:** Surveys, social media mentions, and website traffic.
- **Customer Loyalty:** Repeat purchase rates and Net Promoter Scores (NPS).
- **Engagement:** Likes, shares, and comments on social platforms.

Example: Coca-Cola's consistent branding strategy has made it one of the most recognized brands globally, with a strong emotional connection to its audience.

Exercises and Reflection

Exercises

1. **Brand Audit:** Evaluate your current branding elements. Are they consistent and aligned with your mission?
2. **Persona Creation:** Develop detailed personas for your target audience.
3. **Brand Statement:** Write a concise statement that defines your brand's essence in one sentence.

Reflection Questions

- How does your current branding align with your startup's vision and values?
- What steps can you take to ensure your brand remains authentic and consistent?
- How can your brand story create an emotional connection with your audience?

A strong brand identity is more than a visual or verbal statement—it's the emotional and intellectual bridge between your startup and its audience. By crafting a thoughtful and consistent brand, you can build lasting relationships and establish a competitive edge in the marketplace.

17

The Crescendo – Harmonizing Success, Legacy, and the Exit

In the symphony of entrepreneurship, the finale is both a celebration and a culmination of all the movements that preceded it. This chapter explores how startups can create lasting legacies while navigating the critical stages of exiting, scaling, and sustaining impact. It reflects on the entrepreneurial journey—from the spark of an idea to the final crescendo—and provides actionable insights for crafting a harmonious conclusion to your startup story.

Reflecting on the Journey

Every startup begins with a dream, a vision to solve a problem or bring something unique to the world. The entrepreneurial journey is fraught with challenges, breakthroughs, and moments of triumph. Reflecting on this journey, it's crucial to:

- Celebrate milestones, big and small, that shaped the startup.
- Acknowledge the people—employees, partners, and customers—who contributed to the success.
- Recognize the lessons learned from failures and setbacks.

These reflections not only provide closure but also set the stage for defining the legacy you wish to leave behind.

Moments That Define the Journey

As you reflect, it's worth identifying specific moments that were pivotal:

- **The First Breakthrough:** Recalling the initial success that validated your idea.
- **Overcoming Challenges:** Celebrating times when obstacles seemed insurmountable but were conquered through persistence and innovation.

- **Cultural Milestones:** The day your team came together to solve a major issue or celebrate an achievement.
- **Customer Stories:** Reflecting on how your product or service transformed lives or businesses.

These stories form the narrative of your journey and serve as inspiration for those who will follow in your footsteps.

The Pillars of Sustainable Success

Innovation: The Lifeblood of Startups

Innovation is the engine that drives startups forward. However, sustaining innovation requires:

1. **Continuous Learning:** Stay updated with industry trends and emerging technologies. Attend conferences, read widely, and maintain curiosity about the world.
2. **Customer Feedback:** Use insights from users to refine and expand your offerings. Engage actively through surveys, focus groups, and direct interactions.

3. **Experimentation:** Foster a culture that encourages calculated risks and creative thinking. Build prototypes, pilot new initiatives, and remain open to pivoting when necessary.

Example: Google's consistent investment in moonshot projects, such as self-driving cars and renewable energy, demonstrates how innovation sustains relevance.

Adaptability: Thriving in Change

Markets evolve, customer needs shift, and competitors emerge. Adaptability ensures survival. Strategies include:

- **Scenario Planning:** Anticipate potential disruptions and prepare contingencies for different outcomes.
- **Agile Operations:** Develop processes that allow for quick pivots, such as adopting new technologies or changing target markets.
- **Empowering Teams:** Equip employees with the skills and autonomy to adapt, fostering a proactive approach to problem-solving.

Case Study: Netflix's transition from DVD rentals to streaming services highlights how adaptability can lead to dominance in an evolving market.

People: The Heart of the Symphony

Behind every successful startup is a team that believed in the vision. To build and retain a high-performing team:

1. **Invest in Development:** Provide training, mentorship, and opportunities for growth. Employees who feel valued are more likely to stay committed.
2. **Foster Inclusion:** Create a culture where diverse perspectives thrive, recognizing that innovation often arises from different viewpoints.
3. **Recognize Contributions:** Celebrate achievements and reward excellence. Public acknowledgment of individual and team efforts builds morale and loyalty.

The Entrepreneur as a Conductor

The entrepreneur's role evolves over time, from the creator of ideas to the orchestrator of operations and strategy. To lead effectively:

- **Balance Vision and Execution:** Align long-term goals with day-to-day activities, ensuring that every action contributes to the bigger picture.
- **Communicate Clearly:** Share your vision in ways that resonate with employees, investors, and customers.
- **Delegate Strategically:** Trust your team with responsibilities to focus on broader objectives. Delegation also empowers team members, fostering a sense of ownership.

Leadership Styles That Inspire

Different startups require different leadership approaches. Reflect on how your leadership style evolved over time:

- **Transformational Leadership:** Inspiring and motivating teams to achieve extraordinary results.
- **Servant Leadership:** Prioritizing the needs of the team and fostering a collaborative environment.
- **Adaptive Leadership:** Changing strategies and approaches to meet new challenges.

The Exit: Selling Your Startup

Exiting a startup is a pivotal moment that requires careful planning and execution. Whether through acquisition, merger, or IPO, the exit marks the culmination of your efforts.

Understanding the Exit Process

1. **Types of Exits:**
    - **Acquisition:** Selling the company to a larger organization.
    - **Merger:** Combining forces with another company to create a new entity.
    - **IPO:** Taking the company public by listing shares on a stock exchange.
2. **Why Exit:**
    - To secure financial returns for founders and investors.
    - To leverage resources from a larger entity for growth.
    - To transition to new opportunities.

Preparing for the Sale

A successful exit requires preparation:

- **Financial Health:** Ensure accurate and transparent financial records.
- **Operational Efficiency:** Optimize processes to demonstrate scalability.
- **Market Positioning:** Highlight your competitive advantages and growth potential.
- **Legal Compliance:** Resolve outstanding issues to avoid delays during due diligence.

Negotiating the Deal

1. **Valuing Your Startup:** Work with experts to determine a fair valuation based on revenue, growth, and market trends.
2. **Choosing the Right Buyer:** Assess whether the buyer aligns with your company's vision and values.
3. **Structuring the Agreement:** Define terms, including payment structure, transition roles, and non-compete clauses.
4.

After the Exit

Life beyond the startup can be fulfilling:

- **Philanthropy:** Use your wealth and experience to support causes you're passionate about.
- **Mentorship:** Guide other entrepreneurs on their journeys.
- **New Ventures:** Channel your energy into new ideas or industries.

Example: When Instagram was acquired by Facebook, the founders transitioned to advisory roles while pursuing new creative projects.

Impact Beyond Business

A startup's impact extends beyond profits. By integrating social responsibility and ethical practices, you can:

- **Support Communities:** Engage in initiatives that uplift your stakeholders.
- **Promote Sustainability:** Reduce environmental impact through thoughtful operations.

- **Inspire Others:** Share your story to encourage aspiring entrepreneurs.

Case Study: Patagonia's commitment to sustainability has made it a global leader in ethical business practices.

Building a Legacy

Creating a legacy means defining the enduring contributions of your startup. Steps to achieve this include:

- **Documenting Your Journey:** Share your experiences through books, blogs, or speaking engagements.
- **Fostering Innovation:** Invest in future technologies or startups.
- **Succession Planning:** Prepare the next generation of leaders to carry your vision forward.

Resilience and Reflection

Resilience is the thread that ties the entrepreneurial journey together. Reflecting on challenges and successes:

- Reinforces the lessons learned.

- Highlights the value of persistence and adaptability.
- Provides a sense of closure and fulfillment.

Example: Starbucks' founder Howard Schultz returned during a challenging period to rejuvenate the brand, demonstrating resilience and vision.

Conclusion: The Entrepreneur's Symphony

As the final notes of your startup symphony fade, the impact of your journey will resonate in the lives you've touched and the changes you've inspired. This crescendo is not the end but a transition to new beginnings—a legacy of innovation, leadership, and purpose. Go forward, conduct your symphony, and inspire the world.

****

www.ingramcontent.com/pod-product-compliance
Lightning Source LLC
Chambersburg PA
CBHW050018170726
48282CB00025B/458
* 9 7 8 8 1 9 7 3 6 7 4 1 0 *